Contents

Look for these boxes:

Stay safe
These boxes tell you how to keep yourself and your friends safe from harm.

In your day
These boxes show you how science is a part of your daily life.

Measure up!
These boxes give you some fun facts and figures to think about.

Some words appear in bold, **like this**. You can find out what they mean by looking at the green bar at the bottom of the page or in the glossary.

What's hot? What's not?

A summer day can be sizzling. You step outside and feel the heat. The air and pavement are hot. Sand on a beach and slides in a playground are hot.

Hot summer days make people want to cool down in the water in a pool or at a beach.

Things outdoors can be hot, but so can things indoors. Do you like hot food? Hot soup tastes good. Some drinks are hot. A chocolate drink tastes good when it is hot. Mashed potatoes and macaroni cheese also taste good when they are hot.

THE SCIENCE BEHIND

at

J

Darlene Stille

www.raintreepublishers.co.uk
Visit our website to find out
more information about
Raintree books.

To order:
☎ Phone 0845 6044371
▤ Fax +44 (0) 1865 312263
▦ Email myorders@raintreepublishers.co.uk

Customers from outside the UK please telephone +44 1865 312262

Raintree is an imprint of Capstone Global Library
Limited, a company incorporated in England and
Wales having its registered office at 7 Pilgrim
Street, London, EC4V 6LB – Registered company
number: 6695582

Edited by Megan Cotugno and Laura Knowles
Designed by Richard Parker
Picture research by Mica Brancic
Original Illustrations © Capstone Global Library
   Ltd 2012
Illustrations by Oxford Designers & Illustrators
Originated by Capstone Global Library Ltd
Printed and bound in China by Leo Paper
   Products Ltd

ISBN 978 1 406 23401 5 (hardback)
15 14 13 12 11
10 9 8 7 6 5 4 3 2 1

ISBN 978 1 406 23407 7 (paperback)
17 16 15 14 13
10 9 8 7 6 5 4 3 2 1

British Library Cataloguing in Publication Data
Stille, Darlene R.
The science behind heat.
536-dc22
A full catalogue record for this book is available
from the British Library.

Acknowledgements
We would like to thank the following for
permission to reproduce photographs: NASA
pp. **7** (JPL-Caltech/UCLA), **8** (XRT/Hinode),
© Howard Edin p. **11**; Science Photo Library
p. **6** (Agema Infrared Systems); Shutterstock
pp. **4** (© Eduard Stelmakh), **5** (© Crydo),
9 (© Beboy), **13** (© Ekler), **18** (© A_mikos),
19 (© Marek Cech), **21** (© Geoffrey Kuchera),
23 (© prism68); US Airforce p. **14** (Master
Sergeant Mark W. Fortin).

Cover image of the Sun reproduced with
permission of NASA.

We would like to thank David Crowther and Nancy
Harris for their invaluable help in the preparation
of this book.

Soup getting hot on a kitchen stove smells delicious.

Some things around your house are too hot to touch. Kitchen stoves and toasters can get very hot. Light bulbs get too hot to touch. **Radiators** and electric heaters get very hot.

Other things are not hot. Winter days can be cold. Snow is cold. Lemonade feels cool, and ice cream feels cold. A frozen pizza feels very cold.

radiator   metal pipes that give off heat from hot water inside them to warm a house

What is heat?

Heat is an important type of **energy** (power). **Heat energy** makes things feel hot. Heat energy from one object can move to another object. Heat is a type of energy that makes **temperatures** warm up.

Everything gives off heat. The Sun and other stars in space give off heat. Your body gives off heat. The lamp in your bedroom gives off heat.

An image taken with a special type of camera shows heat coming from a house.

energy   ability to do work
heat energy   form of energy that flows from a hot object to a cooler one

Some things that give off heat also give off light.
The Sun gives off both heat and light.

Special cameras can take pictures of heat coming from objects in space.

In your day

Have you ever held your hand near a toaster when it was toasting bread? Your hand feels warm because the hot toaster gives off heat **rays** that travel through the air. But touching the toaster could burn you!

temperature   measure of heat energy in an object
rays   straight lines that seem to beam from hot objects

What makes heat?

Heat comes from different places and things. One place is the Sun.

The very hot Sun

The Sun is a burning ball of **gas**. Burning gas makes the Sun shine. The surface of the Sun is about 5,500 °Celsius (9,900 °Fahrenheit). That is about 100 times hotter than the hottest place on Earth. Heat and light **rays** blast from the Sun. They travel through space and hit things on Earth. The Sun's rays cause summer days to be hot. The Sun's rays can make pavements and playground slides too hot to touch.

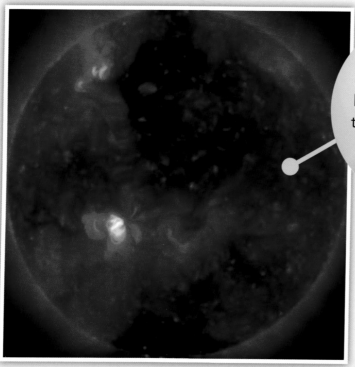

The Sun is a burning ball of gas that sends out heat and light.

gas   vapour that is not a liquid or a solid

Heat from inside Earth

Heat also comes from inside Earth. Deep down inside it is hot enough to melt rock. Sometimes the melted rock shoots up and pours out of a volcano as lava.

Heat inside the Earth also makes water underground very hot. Sometimes the water shoots up out of the ground like a fountain.

The melted rock that pours out of a volcano is called lava.

In your day

Have you ever touched a bike that was left out in the sunshine on a hot day? The Sun's rays can heat up the bike. The metal parts can become too hot to touch. Moving the bike into the shade will cool it off.

Heat from fuels and friction

Heat comes from burning **fuels**. Oil, coal, and natural gas are **fossil fuels**. Fossil fuels come from plants and animals that lived long ago. Heat also comes from burning wood. Wood comes from trees.

Fossil Fuel	Where is it found?	What does it provide heat for?
Coal	Mined from near the surface or deep underground	Electric power stations
Oil	Drilled from rocks underground or under the sea and brought up in oil wells	Houses, factories, power stations, petrol for cars, jet fuel for aeroplanes
Natural gas	Drilled from underground and sent through pipes	Houses, cooking, power plants, natural gas vehicles

Friction also makes heat. Friction comes from rubbing two surfaces together. Striking a match head against a rough surface causes friction. The friction makes enough heat to cause the match to burn.

fuel   material that can be burned to make heat
fossil fuel   material from plants and animals that died millions of years ago

A meteor is a rock that falls from space. Friction between this space rock and the air creates lots of heat.

Heat from electricity

Heat can come from **electricity**. Electricity in homes makes lamps give off heat and light. Electricity in homes can make electric wires in room heaters get very hot. Electricity makes electric stoves hot.

In your day

Have you ever rubbed your hands together when they were cold? Rubbing made them feel warmer. You were making heat by friction.

friction   what happens when you rub one object against another
electricity   form of energy used to make light and heat, and to power machines

How hot is hot?

Have you ever felt ill? Did someone take your **temperature**? He or she probably used a digital **thermometer**. A digital thermometer has a part called a probe that you hold in your mouth. Numbers in a small window show what your body temperature is.

You can use a thermometer to measure the air temperature indoors. Knowing the indoor temperature tells you whether to turn the heat up or down.

Knowing the temperature outdoors helps you decide whether to wear a coat or a T-shirt to school. You could use a thermometer with a dial, or one with a glass tube filled with coloured **liquid**.

Measure up!

There are many types of thermometers. A digital thermometer shows temperature as numbers in a window. A dial thermometer shows temperature as numbers around the dial. A liquid-in-a-tube thermometer shows temperatures as the liquid goes up and down. Use a thermometer to take your temperature, the temperature indoors, and the temperature outdoors. Record the temperatures on one or both scales, Celsius or Fahrenheit.

thermometer   instrument for measuring temperature

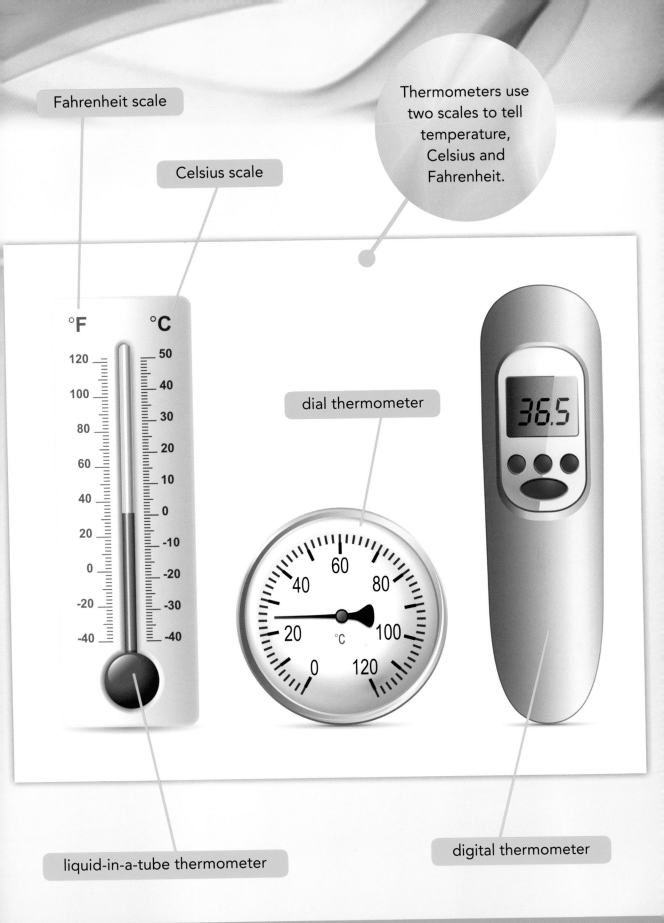

Fahrenheit scale

Celsius scale

Thermometers use two scales to tell temperature, Celsius and Fahrenheit.

°F

°C

dial thermometer

36.5

liquid-in-a-tube thermometer

digital thermometer

liquid   something like water that takes the shape of its container and can be poured

Using heat

You cannot see **heat energy**. You can see the work it does.

Heat for getting around

Cars have engines that burn petrol to make hot **gases**. The hot gases move parts in the engine that make the wheels turn.

Jet aeroplanes burn **fuel** to make hot gases. The hot gases blast out of the jet engine and make the plane move forward.

Hot gases blasting out of a jet engine push the plane forward.

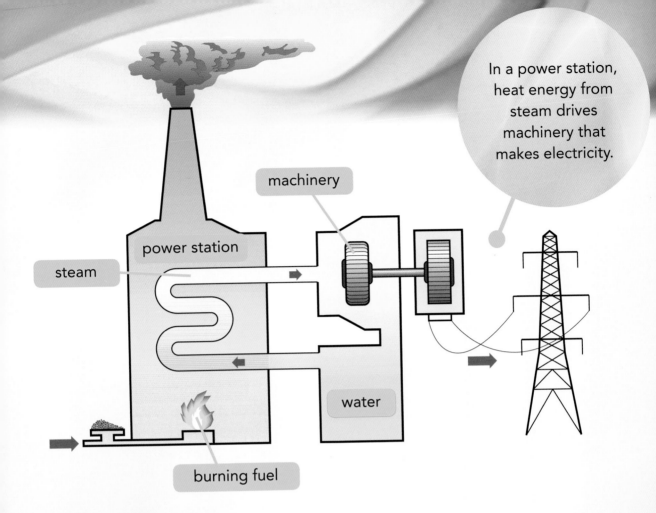

In a power station, heat energy from steam drives machinery that makes electricity.

machinery

power station

steam

water

burning fuel

Heat for making things

Heat energy from burning fuels can change into **mechanical energy** to operate machines in factories. Sometimes this **energy** comes from burning fuels, such as oil, to heat water. The hot water turns to steam, which drives machinery that makes **electricity**.

Stay safe

Do not get burned. Never touch a metal spoon in a pot of hot soup. Heat travels through the metal. Things that give off light, such as candle flames, can also give off heat.

mechanical energy   form of energy linked to motion

Heat cooks

You cook peas in a pot of water on a stove. The burner heats the bottom of the pot. Water touching the pot bottom gets hot. The heat keeps moving through the water. The peas get warm when the heated water touches them and moves through them. Heat moving through objects that touch is called **conduction**.

Heat for baking

You bake bread rolls by putting dough on a baking tray in the oven. A burner heats air in the oven, making the air move. Hot air around the dough bakes the rolls. The movement of hot air in ovens is called **convection**.

Heat from a radiator

Heat **rays** from a **radiator** do not travel through objects. The rays travel through air. Heat from rays is called **radiation**.

In your day

Have you ever tried to cook popcorn in a microwave oven? Microwaves are invisible rays. Microwaves heat water trapped inside corn kernels. The steam makes the kernels explode.

conduction   heat moving through a material
convection   heat moving from hotter to cooler places in a gas or liquid

Heat moves by conduction, convection, and radiation.

Conduction: heat moves through an object

Convection: heat moves by making air or a **liquid** move

Radiation: heat rays move across air or space

radiation   heat rays moving through air or space

Heat changes things

Heat changes **temperatures**. Heat flowing into an object makes the temperature hotter. Heat flowing out makes the temperature cooler.

Heat changes size

When the temperature goes up, a material **expands**, or grows bigger. When the temperature goes down, a material **contracts**, or grows smaller.

A campfire flame creates heat and changes logs into smoke and ash.

expand grow larger
contract get smaller

Heat changes how things look

Heat flowing into a **solid** can change it to a **liquid**. Heat flowing into a liquid can change it to a **gas**. Heat changes ice and water. Ice cubes are solid water. Heating ice cubes turns them into liquid water. Heating liquid water turns it into a gas called water vapour (steam). Burning wood changes it into smoke and ash.

Adding heat causes solid ice to change into liquid water.

Measure up!
Does more heat make ice melt faster? Place an ice cube in a pan at room temperature. Then drop an ice cube into a pan of boiling water. Time how long it takes for both ice cubes to melt.

Heat causes melting

Solid material melts at a certain temperature and turns into a liquid. The **melting point** of ice is 0 °Celsius (32 °Fahrenheit). If there is ice on the pavement, it will melt when the temperature goes above 0 °C (32 °F).

For water, melting and **freezing points** are the same. Liquid water freezes at 0 °C (32 °F). Other materials have higher or lower melting and freezing points.

Melting rock and metal

Rocks can melt because of the high heat inside Earth. It is hard to imagine anything as hot as the melting point of rock. It is between 700 °C and 1,300 °C (1,300 °F and 2,400 °F). The melting point of the metal iron is even higher than rock at 1,535 °C (2,795 °F).

Stay safe
Fingers, toes, ears, and nose can freeze when temperatures are below freezing and the wind is blowing. Wear warm socks, gloves, and a hat during cold winter weather.

melting point   temperature that turns a solid to a liquid
freezing point   temperature where liquid turns to a solid

Metal melted at a high temperature becomes a hot liquid that can be poured.

Holding heat

Heat always flows from hot objects to cooler ones. When you put ice around soft drinks, cold does not flow from the ice into the soft drinks. Heat flows from the soft drinks to the ice.

roof insulation

Insulation goes between the inside and outside walls of a house. It goes between the roof and ceiling.

wall insulation

floor insulation

Insulation

Insulation holds heat inside houses. In winter, it keeps heat in the house from flowing into the cold air outside. Insulation goes inside walls, and under the floor, and roof. Insulation can be sheets of plastic foam. It can be blankets of soft material pushed between boards in the wall. It can be pellets (tiny balls) of these materials blown into the wall.

This man is putting new insulation under a roof.

In your day

You put on a sweater when you feel chilly. The sweater makes you feel warmer. Your sweater is a kind of insulation. It keeps the heat of your body from flowing into the cooler air around your body.

Heat for life

Everything needs just the right amount of heat. The right amount of heat bakes bread rolls. Too much heat can burn the rolls.

You need just the right amount of heat, too. You would freeze if you did not have enough heat. With too much heat, you would cook.

Heating our planet

Earth needs just the right amount of heat. Plants, animals, and people can live on our planet because it is not too hot and not too cold. The **atmosphere** is the **gases** in the air around the planet. Earth's atmosphere works like **insulation**. It holds just the right amount of **heat energy** from the Sun.

If Earth had too much of a certain type of gas, the atmosphere would hold too much heat. Earth's **climate** would change. Some places would grow hotter. There would be more rain, and some places would flood. Other places would become deserts.

atmosphere the gases in air around Earth
climate the kind of weather that a place has year after year

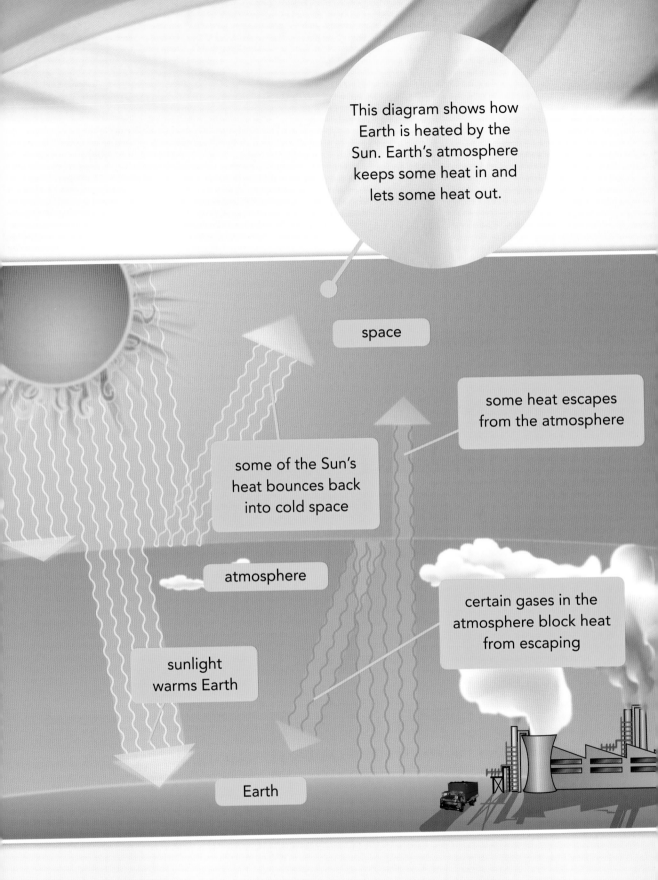

Try it yourself

Sunlight snacks

Here is a tasty treat you can make on a hot summer day using **heat energy** from the Sun.

What you need

- 4 chocolate digestive biscuits
- 12 mini marshmallows or 2 regular marshmallows
- an oven-proof glass baking dish
- a clear glass lid for the baking dish
- an outdoor **thermometer**

What to do

1. Check that the outdoor **temperature** is at least 30 °Celsius (85 °Fahrenheit).
2. place the four chocolate digestives on the bottom of the glass baking dish.
3. Put one regular marshmallow or six mini marshmallows on two of the biscuits.
4. Cover the dish with a clear glass lid.
5. Put the dish outside in a place where full sunlight will shine on it.
6. Leave the dish in the sunlight until the chocolate and marshmallows melt.

7. Put the digestive biscuits chocolate-side-down on top of the marshmallow-covered biscuits, like making a sandwich. You will have two sunlight snacks, one for you and one for a friend.

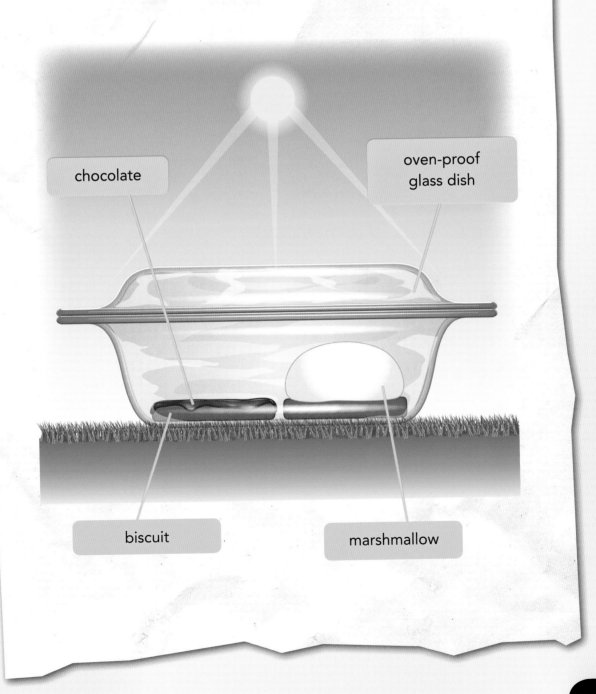

chocolate

oven-proof glass dish

biscuit

marshmallow

Glossary

atmosphere the gases in air around Earth

climate kind of weather that a place has year after year

conduction heat moving through a material

contract get smaller

convection heat moving from hotter to cooler places in a gas or liquid

electricity form of energy used to make light and heat, and to power machines

energy ability to do work

expand grow larger

fossil fuel material from plants and animals that died millions of years ago

freezing point temperature where liquid turns to a solid

friction what happens when you rub one object against another

fuel material that can be burned to make heat

gas vapour that is not a liquid or a solid

heat energy form of energy that flows from a hot object to a cooler one

insulation material that protects against the loss of heat

liquid something like water that takes the shape of its container and can be poured

mechanical energy form of energy linked to motion

melting point temperature that turns a solid to a liquid

radiation heat rays moving through air or space

radiator metal pipes that give off heat from hot water inside them to warm a house

rays straight lines that seem to beam from hot objects

solid something you can hold because it has its own shape

temperature measure of heat energy in an object

thermometer instrument for measuring temperature

Find out more

Use these resources to find more fun and useful information about the science behind heat.

Books

Global Warming (Protect Our Planet), Angela Royston (Heinemann Library, 2009)

Heat (Energy in Action), Ian F. Mahaney (Rosen, 2007)

Hot and Cold (Now You Know Science), Terry Jennings (Franklin Watts, 2009)

Secrets of Heat and Cold (Science Secrets), Andrew Solway (Franklin Watts, 2011)

Understanding Global Warming with Max Axiom (Graphic Science), Agnieszka Biskup (Raintree, 2010)

Websites

www.brainpop.co.uk/science/formsandresources/ heat/preview.weml
Go to the Brain Pop website to discover more about heat and how it is created.

www.brainpop.co.uk/science/formsandresources/ fossilfuels/preview.weml
Learn more about fossil fuels on this website.

www.kidsgeo.com/geography-for-kids/0061- transferring-heat.php
Go to this web page to find out more about heat and heat transfer.

www.sciencemuseum.org.uk/ClimateChanging/ ClimateScienceInfoZone
Visit this Science Museum website to find out why Earth's climate is heating up.

Index

MALPAS
1-8-13.